THE MASS

Malco Kids

Written by
Sr. Karen Cavanagh, CSJ

Illustrations by
Edward Letwenko

Regina
Press

We are one family...

Baptism brings each of us into God's family. We belong to each other and pray together.

Each Sunday at Mass families come together and celebrate that they are all God's family. This celebration is called the Eucharist.

The priest welcomes us and we make the Sign of the Cross as the Mass begins.

We celebrate...

When we celebrate the Lord's day with God's family, Jesus is with us in a special way.

Flowers and candles are signs of celebration and bring color and light to the altar.

Music and song add to our celebration. When we sing of God's goodness, it's like praying twice.

We sing glory to God and we ask God's grace and blessing on our celebration and each other.

We are forgiven...

We do not always work for peace. As Mass begins, we say we are sorry and ask for God's forgiveness.

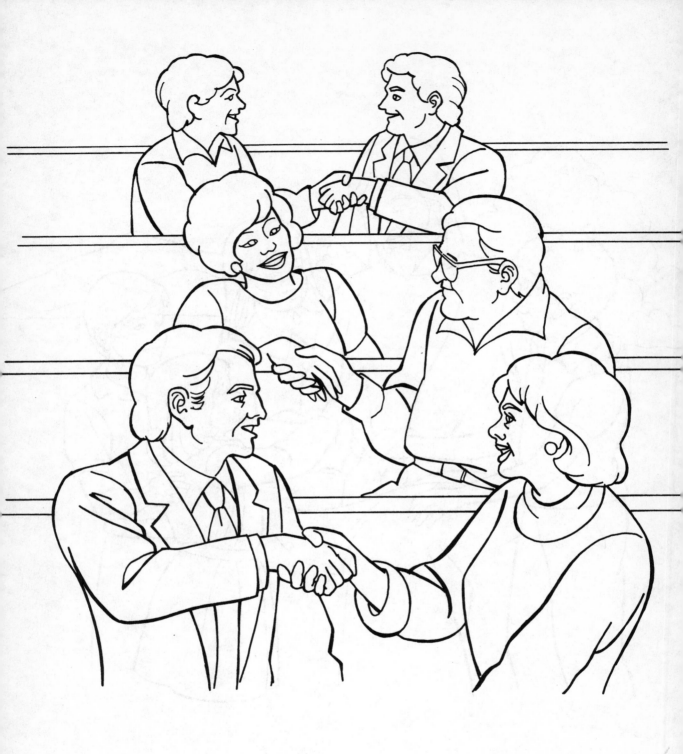

God always forgives. We give each other a greeting as a sign that we are at peace with one another.

When all people live peacefully in the world, we bring about God's kingdom. We pray for this when we say the "Our Father."

We hear God's Word...

When the Word of God is carried into the church, we welcome it with great joy. We sing: Alleluia! Alleluia!

The Lector reads from the Old Testament and from special letters to the early church. We hear stories and poems of God's goodness.

We listen to God's message and think about how we can live out the message.

The Gospel is the good news of Jesus' life, death and resurrection.
The priest speaks of this good news in the Homily.

At each Mass we remember Jesus' last su
took bread and wine, blessed it and shar
same and to always remember him.

with His friends and apostles. He
with them. He asked us to do the

We show care and concern...

God's loving care for each of us shows us how we are able to care for others. We are a family.

We say special prayers for people who care for us. We ask God to bless them and help them.

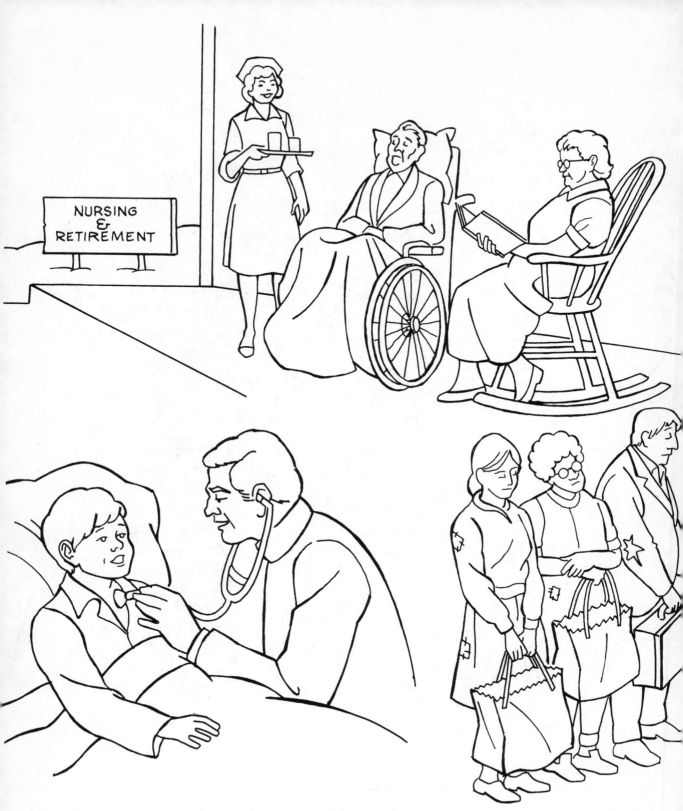

We are reminded of many who are in need of our prayers, care and concern. We ask God to bless them.

At the Eucharist, we give some of our money to help our church and to aid our brothers and sisters who need our help.

We are thankful for God's gifts...

We bring gifts and offerings to the altar because we know that everything we have is a gift from God.

When the priest offers the gifts of bread and wine for us, we also offer ourselves to God.

The world is full of God's glory. We sing, "Holy, Holy, Holy..." in thanksgiving for all God's creations.

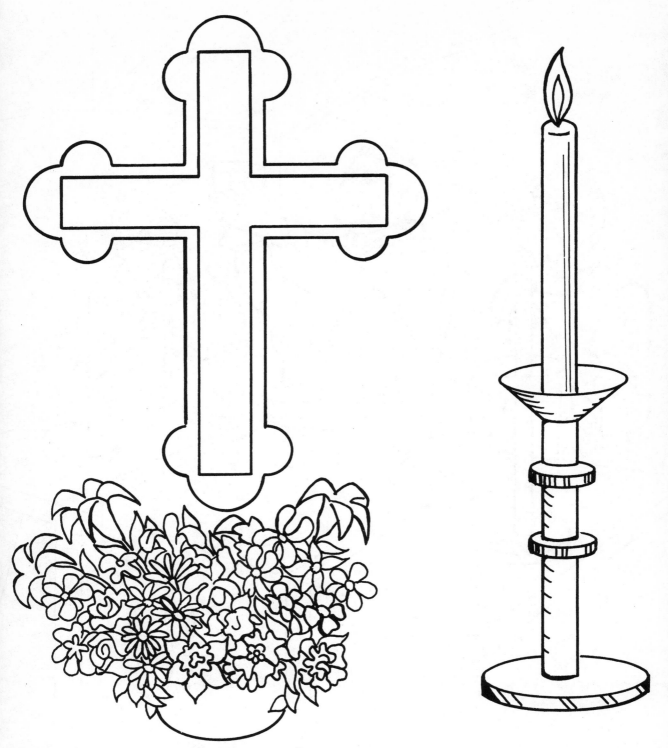

We have new life through Jesus.....

The Cross and Paschal Candle remind us that at every Eucharist we celebrate Easter. Jesus gave His life for us and rose to share new life with us.

Jesus asks us to be partners in His sacrifice by dying for our selfish ways and sharing in God's life. We say: "Amen! Amen!" - "Yes! Yes!"

We share in a meal...

At Communion time, Jesus invites us to share in a special meal. We bring all that we are and all that we do to the Lord's table.

Jesus said, "I am the bread of life." We receive "the Body of Christ." We answer: "Amen!" It means, "Yes, Lord, we believe in You."

The bread and wine are signs of life and unity in God's family. We receive "the blood of Christ." We answer: "Amen!" It means, "Yes, Lord, we believe."

We are sent to build God's Kingdom...

Before we leave the church, the priest blesses us. He prays that we may love and serve God each day as we care for one another.

We sing as God's family going forth in love and friendship to build God's kingdom. We are the builders.

I go to Mass...

Draw your own picture of Sunday Mass in your church and write your own prayer.

_____

_____

_____

_____